Would You Like a Joke?

Book 6

I0085820

A 'Dad Joke' collection

Dave Anderson

Copyright – Disclaimer

These jokes are intended to be enjoyed and shared by the readers. Please do not try to profit directly from the use of this original material.

DISCLAIMER: All jokes originate with the Author. Any joke heard elsewhere is coincidental.

Introduction

With a twinkle in his eye, and a smirk on his face, everyone knew a joke was on the way. This is how my father introduced me to the world of humor. His mother introduced her family to humor, and it was shared by Glen and his five sisters.

His two younger sisters were well practiced in the craft. When the girls got going, they could keep the family laughing for hours. Precious family memories.

The goal of this book, is to give the readers some jokes that they can enjoy, and share with others. Humor and laughter are good medicine.

ENJOY!

Acknowledgments

Most parents agree: parents should embarrass their children. My children say that I took the embarrass idea to the extreme. Admittedly, that is probably true. All the while, I was perfecting my ability to tell jokes. It helped me realize that seeing people laugh is what truly gives me happiness.

As I deliver pizza, my Manager gives me the freedom to offer my customers a joke at the door. This has allowed me to practice and refine my jokes, while providing a more personal service than normal and expected.

Dedication

My Permanent Duty Assignment (USAF) was the 318 FIS (Fighter Interceptor Squadron). The 318th was located at McChord AFB, Tacoma, Washington. I arrived at McChord in March of 1975.

I knew that I wanted to attend a local Church in Tacoma. I looked in the Yellow Pages and found Evergreen Baptist Church (BGC). The Church was nearby, so I called the number. The exact conversation is not recalled, but the Pastor picked me up the next Sunday morning. He took me to Church, then took me back to Base after the morning Service.

After a number of weeks, Pastor Jim and his wife, Brenda Lee, invited me to join their own family for the day. It soon became a standing invitation from Pastor Jim and Brenda Lee. On Sundays, I became a member of their family.

I grew up (some may dispute that fact) on a farm near the small town of Summit, South Dakota. Over the years the population of Summit is normally somewhere between 250 and 300. By all accounts, that is a small town. When my older sister was in College in Saint Paul, MN, she once sent a letter addressed to: "Mom, Dad and Dave, 57266." The letter was delivered to our rural mail box.

In a community of that size, there is not much for young people to do. Of course, there are High School sports, including basketball, football, track and field. There is also music, like choir and band.

As a farm boy, farm chores are a big part of the normal daily, weekly and annual activities. Add to this, weekly Church attendance. By some accounts, I was living a sheltered and naive life.

But now I was out in the big, wide World. In the U S Air Force, nonetheless. There were many choices available to me. Perhaps I KNEW I needed some guidance from those who had more maturity. Or perhaps God was taking Care of me.

This is why I was Blessed to be taken care of by Pastor Jim and Brenda Lee. This new 'family' helped me navigate my Air Force Enlistment with good Spiritual grounding.

Over the years, I lost contact with Pastor Jim and Brenda Lee. Life goes on. Thanks to social media, I was able to reconnect with Pastor Jim and Brenda Lee.

Sadly, Pastor Jim passed away in January, 2021. After over 60 years of marriage, Pastor Jim and Brenda Lee created an amazing legacy. They have six children, 16 grandchildren and (by the time you read this) six great-grandchildren. Of course, the countless lives touched by this couple, in their years in the Ministry, is beyond my ability to ever know.

When I needed stability in my life, Pastor Jim and Brenda Lee were there. God Bless you Jim and Brenda Lee!

1

Why was the yoyo going up and down?

Someone was pulling its string.

2

How did the Soldier lose a fingernail and a tooth?

They were fighting tooth and nail.

3

Why was the crow in trouble, when the liar was found out?

They had to eat crow.

4

Why was it a bright, sunny day at the beach?

The coast was clear.

5

Why did the person NOT drive 30 miles to cross the river?

It was a bridge too far.

6

Why did the male deer stop to see the President?

He heard the President say, "The buck stops here."

7

The Appliance Manufacturing Company employee was moved to Kitchen Appliances. Why were they worried about that?

They thought their career was toast.

8

How do we know the dog toy was clean?

It was squeaky clean.

9

Why did the blacksmith crank up their forge blower?

They had a lot of irons in the fire.

Before going on the first date, why did the person carefully examine their feet?

So they could put their best foot forward.

11

Why was the person sad, when there was a second full moon in the month?

It made them blue.

12

Why did the person avoid the cookout?

They didn't want to get grilled.

13

What is the favorite food of the percussionist?

Drum sticks.

14

How do I know your bed is not real?

You told me you just made it up.

15

What did one blood vessel say to the other blood vessel?

You're so vein.

16

How did COVID-19 cause the couple to divorce?

Their differences were unmasked.

17

After a day of making firewood, what was the state of the lumberjack?

They had a splitting head-ache.

18

Why did the oil change technician try to avoid working downstairs?

It's the pits!

19

Why did the cabinet-maker fail to introduce their new style?

They didn't have it all together.

20

Why was the string all wound up at the stadium?

It was inside baseball.

21

Why does the prosecutor keep eating pudding?

They are always looking for the proof.

22

How are a surgeon and comedian alike?

They both keep you in stitches.

23

Why did the negotiator always do Business in the kitchen showroom?

They wanted to have counter offers available.

24

While climbing out from the airport, what did the pilot say?

The sky is the limit.

25

Why did the clock start to talk?

Time WILL tell.

26

When hanging sheets out to dry, why did the person never hang more than two sheets?

They didn't want to have more than two sheets to the wind.

27

Riddle time: How are an orchestra, a train, and an electrician alike?

They work with conductors.

28

When the wind blew, why did it seem like all of the houses were in a chorus?

They all chimed in.

29

Why did the bacteria feel like it was being scrutinized?

It was under the microscope.

30

How do we know the Arizona forest
was scared to death?

It was petrified.

To be continued. . .

The Power of Humor

This space is normally where I relate a story of how humor led to an amazing conversation. This time, however, I will give you the challenge to 'use' humor to make your life better.

Whenever you can work a joke into conversations, you will find some amazing things happen in your life.

Make sure to use a good joke. A 'good' joke is not too long, can be understood by a wide range of ages, and is not offensive to anyone. While I believe the jokes in this series of books are all 'good' jokes, use any joke that meets these criteria. You will notice these criteria have only positive possible outcomes.

If you are a sales Professional, this could possibly be the difference between making the sale, or not making the sale. At the very least, your potential client will more likely listen to what you have to say. As you continue to 'follow up' they will more likely take your call, or give you time. They may even tell you about their experience telling 'your' joke to others (which will build positive rapport very quickly).

As you conduct your personal business, having a joke will always be welcomed. Virtually everyone is thirsty for good humor, and they will appreciate your effort to make their day better.

In your personal relationships, your friends and family are also looking for good humor. If the jokes in this series of books are not exactly the style that fits your relationships, find some that DO fit. Everyone appreciates an opportunity to laugh and enjoy the company of those they are with.

Finally, in all of these situations, sharing a joke WILL make you memorable. Others will remember you, and they WILL remember you with happy thoughts. What could be better?

Thank you!

We have many choices in our World these days. Thank you for choosing this book. It is hoped that you enjoyed it, and my unique brand of humor.

To contact Dave, email
summitdave56@yahoo.com

To find more books in this series, for tips for Sales Professionals and to see other projects, visit
www.summitdave.com

Expect a new book periodically.

This book marks the halfway point toward the next goal.

Biography

Dave Anderson was raised on a farm near Summit, South Dakota. He was introduced to jokes and humor by his father, Glen. When they saw that particular smirk and grin, everyone knew Glen was telling a joke. This was passed on to Dave and his siblings.

After High School, Dave joined the U S Air Force, being stationed in Tacoma, Washington. After the four-year enlistment, Dave attended College and attained a B A.

Dave landed in Milwaukee, Wisconsin, raising a daughter and son. Delivering pizza, he developed the service of offering a joke to his customers. Creating his own jokes, his customers suggested that he write a book. This continues the 'Dad Joke' series.

www.ingramcontent.com/pod-product-compliance
Lightning Source LLC
Chambersburg PA
CBHW070206060426
42445CB00033B/1684